Poetry With A Twist
Jacqueline James

PUBLISHED by PARABLES
Earthly Stories with a Heavenly Meaning

Poetry With A Twist
Copyright ©Jacqueline James
June, 2018

Published By Parables
June, 2018

All Rights Reserved. No part of this book may be reproduced or utilized in any form or by any means, electronic or mechanical, including photocopying, recording, or by any information storage and retrieval system, without permission in writing from the author.

Unless otherwise specified Scripture quotations are taken from the authorized version of the King James Bible.

Readers should be aware that Internet Web sites offered as citations and/or sources for further information may have been changed or disappeared between the time this was written and when it is read.

Illustration provided by www.unsplash.com

ISBN 978-1-945698-56-9

Printed in the United States of America

Poetry With A Twist
Jacqueline James

Table of Content.

General
1. Family — 8
2. Unknown — 9
3. They're lost — 10
4. Cloned — 11

Spiritual
1. 1st prayer — 16
2. Jesus — 18
3. Christmas Joy — 20
4. Help me — 21
5. God's Army — 23
6. He reigns — 25
7. God's puppet — 27
8. His Birth — 29

Educational
1. The set — 32
2. Forgiveness — 34
3. Obey — 35
4. Cocaine rules - the 'Hell' you say! — 37

Informative
1. Lead on — 41
2. The gift — 43
3. I see you — 45
4. If — 46
5. Save yourself — 47
6. Children — 51
7. If I must — 52
8. Resilience — 54
9. Time — 55
10. The Journey — 57
11. Race — 59

12. Just passing through	61
13. Sex games	63
14. Loyalty	66
15. Now, now, now	68
16. Strang-er	70

Entertainment

1. Love called	73
2. Trapped	75
3. Out of control	76
4. Puppy Love	77
5. Patient	79
6. Cook it	80
7. The ex	83
8. Her beauty	85
9. Purple	87
10. The loaner	88
11. Friends	90
12. New Life	92
13. Passion	94

Special Dedication

1. 47 years of Love	98
2. Grammie-son	100
3. Magic girl	102
4. My 1st	104
5. Grandmother	105
6. 2 Hearts	107
7. What a friend	109
8. Celebration	111
9. Disguised	112
10. Miracle son	114
11. God Bless	116
12. Mother	117
13. Chosen	118
14. Breaking bridges	120

About the Author

Jacqueline James is the youngest of four children born in the mid-60s during the time of the 'Black Revolution', and the freedom marches. She was raised in St Louis Missouri in the heart of the city through a middle-class family. She became a mother at a very young age, which led her to alternative education. She completed a trade in word processing, at St Louis Job Corps where she also obtained her GED. Afterward, she attended St. Louis Community College. Later she extended her family with four additional children and married.

Her first husband preceded her in death. She worked as a home health care provider for elderly and disabled clients. She has a great passion for cooking, which led her to work over the years as a chef at their family restaurant. And she continues to cook to this day for each one of their family events. She has also satisfied several catering events, for private parties over the years as well. She's is well known, and loved for her authentic recipes. Jacqueline later remarried and threw that Union acquired an infant stepson. Jacqueline and her husband purchased a resale shop, and a hauling company, which he worked at on a daily basis. While she was a stay-at-home mom. By the time her stepson reached school age, she divorced. Afterward, her life would take her on an amazing journey.

While her children were coming into their adulthood, attending college, and finding their own way in life. Jacqueline begins to express her natural gift in poetry. Jacqueline never learned to type, however she found a unique way to overcome her shortcomings by using talk-to-text on her cellphone.

Then she would email each poem to herself, edit them on the word document on her computer, then print them. Jacqueline has written several poems over the years during her leisure.

However, God has blessed her with the peace and admiration to fulfill her dreams in a beautiful expression of writing, to become a published author.

Jacqueline is a Christian field woman and is an active member in the Church of God in Christ, she's loved by all who meets and greet her. She has a forever given spirit, who's a very influential person. To know her is to love her, and to accept her charm immediately into your heart. She brings lots of talent and enthusiasm to her writing. Her ultimate goal through her poetry is to reach a mass audience, to motivate, and inspire them with her poems, and allow them to share with her the 'joy', in her Christian walk.

The Dedication

This book is dedicated to my mother Jeanette L. Whitehorn who has always believed in me and my ability to achieve, and conquer whatever was put before me through the grace of God.

Thank you mama for your discipline, and guidance, and raising me with strong Christian values, I appreciate you for instilling in me the confidence, and a realistic approach in life to work hard with strong convictions to follow my dreams.

You've inspired me to work with devotion, and with honesty and integrity to complete any possible task, put before me.

I love you very much, and I thank God that you're alive to see my achievement!!!

Introduction

This book of poetry is written by a Christian Author inspired both by fiction and nonfiction events.

Jacqueline James compose lots of general life experiences of her own and others around.

And uniquely captured their essence, composing them into a marvelous one-of-a-kind collection of poetry. She has written them so cleverly to capture, inspire, educate, inform, amuse, and comfort her audience, by bringing to them something that not only can they relate to, but can find a sense of self, within her words:

The poems Jacqueline has written will lure every and all race, creed, color, and ethnicity.

They will appeal to every age and walks of life as well.

There's no limits or restrictions on how many lives that will be inspired, as well as possibly influence through her writing.

God has truly unleashed a blessing of creativity through Jacqueline candid talent, expressed in the pages of this book.

She is set on a mission with one objective on this journey, and that's to bring to you, fulfillment, satisfaction, and a great sense of awareness while she continuously entertains, you through poem, after poem, after poem.

POETRY WITH A TWIST

Chapter 1
General
1. Family
2. Unknown
3. They're lost
4. Cloned

Family...
What my family means to me;
Look around and you will see;
From the old and to the new, all the love is shining through;
Rushing through the ocean shore; forceful as a lion's roar;
We stick together in a pack;
Stopping the world, in it's track:
We laugh, we cry, we sing, we play;
When it's all over, we did it our way!

Unknown...

Sitting, Waiting, anticipating;
Something extraordinary, or out of the ordinary;
My will to submit to its presence is overwhelming;
I long for its insatiable relief with delight;
Needing desperately to break the monotonous of the day;
Finding annoyance in every gesture that's announced;
Mesmerized by the fantasy of it captivating my attention and sending me soaring into a dissolute state of mind:
Will its surroundings expire a stitch in which unpleasantly repulse me -to a point of regurgitation?;
Or am I to embrace its aroma with fulfillment, such as the gentleness of the evening spray!?
Will it's vibration roar through with the energy of a volcano, and break my solitude?;
Or will it whisper by so delicately, as calm as an infant's breath?
I'm imagining the intensity of a touch, with the textures smooth, and soothing like a silk scarf across my face;
Preoccupied by the phantom that consumes me;
My disposition torn by the thought of it possibly being pleasing to my eyes;
So all the day, the evening I'll wait... and on through the night:

They're Lost...

I usually smile, and wave at the people I greet;
Some are very unpleasant, that I meet:
People don't even want to speak to you anymore;
They won't even show common courtesy, or hold open the door:
What is this world coming to?
When we can't find the civil thing to do:
Always rushing here and there;
End up not going anywhere:
Needing to be important by staying busy;
Their confusion makes us all dizzy:
Caught up in self-loathing situation;
Making the simplest things complicated:
Refusing to show common courtesy;
Even when the events calls for urgency:
Lacking empathy and that's for sure;
Not even for the innocence, who's hearts are pure:
They have no clue how to sympathize;
Although it's warranted, before their eyes:
This generation of people stay on a hype;
Drawing their own conclusions from the night:
Desiring to be flamboyant or just noticed at all;
However lacking confidence, and continuously feeling small:

JACQUELINE JAMES

They walk around like the "Living Dead";
Trying to find an escape from the things in their head
Their life's are over, even before they before they began;
Because they don't have Jesus as their spiritual friend:
It's not too late, it's really okay;
If they just take the time to repent and pray:
I'm leaving you'll with this message because;
I don't want you to leave this earth with your soul's lost:
Give your life to Christ he'll change your thoughts:
Your burdens will be lifted, and that's no doubt:
He paid for our sins on that old rugged cross:
So pray right now, and God will forgive you;
It's the right, and the Christian thing to do:

Cloned...

Before I was born I came from dirt;
God breathe into my soul, right at birth:
My destiny is clear, it's not an illusion;
My existence through time, will draw its own conclusions:
I'm one of a kind, and can't be duplicated;
Everything about me is authenticated:
You can take my body's DNA;
But it can't be cloned anyway:
I'm all natural, I'm not fake;
Whatever's necessary, I'll do what it take:
I'll continue to strive throughout my life;
To prove I'm worthy, is a constant fight:
If you try to 'mock' me it's okay;
I can't be copied anyway:
Whatever I say, or do is all original;
I can't explain it, is very mystical:
I'll reveal God's miracle, before your eyes;
When I share my gift with the world, then you'll realize:
I'm much more than a falling star;

JACQUELINE JAMES

My light is to be admire, from afar:
I know you all want to clone a piece of me;
But it's impossible, cause my soul is free:
Someone's always trying to steal my style;
If you're in search of replica, you'll be searching for a while:
I don't know exactly how this all came to be;
I know God granted me with a gift of an epiphany:
So if you copy, or try to reproduce;
You'll get something unusual, with no excuse:

POETRY WITH A TWIST

Chapter 2

Spiritual
1. 1st prayer
2. Jesus
3. Christmas Joy
4. Help me
5. God's Army
6. He reigns
7. God's puppet
8. His Birth

1st Prayer...

Sorrow is a bird with a broken wing;.
I lift my hearts to Jesus, now I sing:
Grace be unto me, my merciful Lord;
My life without you, is painful and hard:
I acknowledge you in everything I say, and do;
You're here for comfort, to see me through:
The Joy you bring, to each of my days;
Humbles my spirit, and changes my ways:
This perfect peace, the world could never give;
For you I'll die, and for you I'll live:
My heart is filled with love and content;
From God's only begotten son, he sent:
You forgave me over, and over, for the things I've done;
That's why you sent your only son:
I'll praise him now, for that's my choice;
I'll give him honor, when I lift my voice:
I worship him throughout my day;
I call his name, as I pray:
I'll always love you, because you first loved me;
As I give you the glory, it's your reflection I see:
I need you Lord to continue to guide me;
With your deliverance, my soul is free:
Come in my heart, and examine it please;
Whatever's not worthy, remove it with ease:

JACQUELINE JAMES

My desire is to serve you for the rest of my days;
To honor you Father, when I sing with praise:
Keep my lips worthy to call your name;
Throughout my struggle, there'll be no pain:
Cover me with your precious blood;
Let my cup run over from all your love:
Surely you know what's right for me;
I may not always understand, but you clearly see:
Nevertheless, you are my rock;
And that alone I'll never doubt:
You are a healer, and a doctor as well;
The miracles you conquer, I can't wait to tell:
Keep me strong to fight in your army;
My days may be long, but Joy cometh in the morning:
You're always there when I need you the most;
Because I believe, it separates me from other folks:
Lord my prayer is to be closer to you;
Help me Father live it though:

Jesus...

When I was sick, and in the hospital;
I wasn't worried because God was in the middle:
I know who my father is, and I know his power;
He comes to heal, at any hour:
He sent his angels to comfort me;
The smiles and laughter, were the best remedy:
I appreciate all the visitors prayers, gifts and cards;
All the love and concern, it wasn't nothing but the Lord:
Jesus filled my room with love right from the start:
He wanted to heal my body, and mend some hearts;
My body was tired, and needed some rest;
So he slowed me down to recuperate, so I'll do my best:
While lying in the bed, I couldn't hardly move;
I had no choice but to let God shine through:
The vision became clear what he wanted from me; my writing;
my poems;
were my destiny!

This will come to me as no shock;
because without full expression, I was putting my own light out:
I love the Lord because he first loved me;
And if he can give up his life,
I can accept him molding me into the Christian, I need to be:
And I thank you Jesus for all you've done;
Because seeing their reactions is so much fun:
I never realize how powerful words can be;
they can change life's, and allow eyes to see:
And on this path, is where I choose to stay;
At the end of my journey I'll see God's face one day:

Christmas Joy...

Three wise men traveled throughout the night;
They followed the star, that shone so bright;
It came upon us a baby boy, and to the earth he brought forth Joy:
He was born in a manger in an old horse barn;
He was sent from God; King of Kings and Lord of lords:
His mission was to lighting our loads:
To cure our sick bodies and to save our souls:
He's our shepherd born on Christmas Day;
To lead us through the darkness and help us find our way:
His mother would be a virgin girl, her name was Mary, known
throughout out the world;
His birth was prophesized in Isaiah 7:14;
He would be our Messiah, he will be our King!
Jesus walked this Earth 33 years as a man and
he was crucified and died,
God shook the earth with a loud roar, and when he hung his head-
the heavens cried!
And in 3 days he rose from his grave;
Given all mankind who believed, the of power of the Holy Ghost
to be saved:

Help me...

Ain't nobody gonna help me but Jesus;
He died for that very reason:
He loved me before I even knew myself:
Without his grace, I wouldn't have nothing left:
He never turned his back, like most folks;
He's always there, when I need him the most:
It doesn't bother him when I scream, vent, or cry;
He never judges me, or ask me why:
He knows my thoughts and he knows my heart;
He knows I was humble, right from the start:
I love him, because he first loved me;
And I'll embrace this love spiritually:
He always helped me find my way;
Despite the things, I do or say:
I thank you Lord for helping me;
And given me peace, from the things I see:
I'll never deny you, and that's for sure;
Your love is peace, your love is pure:
You dried up all my tears you know;
And lightning my load, when I had far to go:
You washed away my sins, over, and over again;
I know in my heart, you are my true friend:

You shed your blood, and was crucified;
And rose again to testify:
I thank you Jesus for loving me;
Because of your grace I've been set free:
You've lifted all my burdens off;
With your life you paid the cost:
God, I could never thank you enough, for what you've done;
When you gave your only begotten son;
By Faith I'm strong, and that's for real;
And as a Christian, I choose to live;
You're much more than my eyes can see;
And I love you to infinity:

God's Army...

Fight the good fight, for salvation and righteousness;
Stay humble in search of God's greatness:
The mink is the one's to inherit the earth;
We must all be transformed, through rebirth:
Baptism through the Holy Ghost that's how we're born again:
And accepting Jesus in a heart as our savior and friend:
Now we must all fight a spiritual warfare;
To gain salvation, while we're here:
You need to be properly suited for the fight;
And humble yourself to see Jesus light:
With the buckle of truth around your waist;
You'll stand strong when there's evil in this world to face:
Put on the breastplate of righteousness for your next move;
God will make sure your battle goes smooth:
Step your feet into a temperament of peace;
This will insure you a life of ease:
Studying the bible makes God's word your sword;
Store it in your heart and the war won't be hard:
Put on the helmet of salvation to free your soul;
When you're suited for battle, God's in control:
With your shield of faith you'll never doubt;
That God's love will always bring you out:

When you worship together with other saints dressed the same;
You know that you're fighting a good fight in Jesus name:
When we join together, we form God's army;
We'll fight with love and peace in perfect harmony:

He Reigns...

When the darkness come I don't fear;
It's because of God's grace, that I'm here:
He reigned over me and my life;
He shed his blood, with a sacrifice:
It was paid in full on that rugged cross;
My sins was washed, when his life was lost:
He's a God of another chance;
Through the power prayer, his mercy will last:
Let his peace reign down over me;
Through unconditional love, his light I'll see:
He's blood works miracles through my day;
My cup runneth over, as I pray:
When sickness come, through faith I'm healed;
The world can see, my Lord is real:
He keeps me safe, in the mist of my storm;
I'm in perfect peace, cradled in his arms:
I can't thank him enough for all he's done;
He fought the enemy, and for me he won:
The battle isn't over, we're in a spiritual warfare;
God's sticking closely, because he care:
He reigns with mercy, and strengthen me;
My chains were loosened, and I'm set free:
My life is full from all he gives;
And nothing but peace, do I feel:

He blessed my generations to come as well;
So they'll all have a story of his grace to tell:
We all know that God words are powerful, and strong;
They'll reign truth over our life's, and we're never alone:
If you want God miracles for yourself;
Then except him as your savior, while you still have breath:
You must open your heart, to receive his love;
He'll reign out blessings, from above:

God's Puppet...

I beat to his drum, I pray at his feet;
I share his love with the people I greet:..
I'm his puppet on a string;
For his love, I lift my voice and sing:
I worship Him throughout my days;
He controls my mind, and my praise:
He orders my thoughts, and my speech;
He controls the dance in my feet:
He chooses my path, that I walk;
He controls my words, when I talk:
He keeps my soul longing for more;
For his mercy, is what I live for:
He shows me his amazing grace;
He keeps a smile, on my face:
I worship and praise on his command;
I write poetry for him, on demand:
He makes sure my faith don't cease;
By keeping me in his perfect peace:
From his life, he gives his will;
In my days, the hope I feel:
Now I'm his puppet on a string;
As a Christian, I'll do my thing:
The Lord is my shepherd, guiding me through;
To God's love, I know it's true:

He keeps me happy and satisfied;
He forgives my sins, he don't deny:
'To your will be done', in my life -- my Lord;
For your acceptance I'll work hard:
I'm your puppet on a string;
I'll serve you always, my Holy King:
He lifts my arms with his praise;
He keeps me strong through my days:
He helps me up, when I stand;
I give him The Glory, and clap my hands:
He lets me love, even when I don't want to;
He teaches me the righteous things to do:
He humbles my spirit and brings me Joy;
I'm his puppet, I'm his "Toy":
He helps me every day I live;
He keeps me safe, with his comfort, I feel:
He keeps my mind, set on him;
He renews my faith, so my light's not dim:
I'm blessed that God does all the work for me;
Through his deliverance, my soul is free:
God I'm your puppet on a string;
I'm here to serve you-you are my King:

His Birth...

I have good news to share and tell;
Our savior was born today, his name is Immanuel:
Thank you, Jesus, for being born today;
Because of your Grace, I can find my way
God, you sent us all your only begotten son;
If the world search for a higher King, there is none:
He came to forgive us from our sins;
To bring us peace, to be our friend:
He walked the earth saving and healing his people;
Filling them with love of the Holy Ghost
to worship he his temples:
After being rejected and crucified;
Jesus shed his blood, he gave his life:
Don't let his death be in vein:
Accept him in your life, in your heart as your savior,
make a change:
Thank you, Jesus, for your birth, your death, and your resurrection;
Though your love and peace, we've all connected;

Poetry With A Twist

Chapter 3
Educational
1. The set
2. Forgiveness
3. Obey
4. Cocaine rules - the 'Hell' you say!

The Set...

Are we products of Dr. Martin Luther King
just staying neutral waiting on a dream?
Are we descendants of Malcolm X ready to retaliate on sure facts?
Why are our people somewhere loading a gun?
When the rest of the world is working going about their lives, and
occasionally having fun?
What should we teach our children?
What exactly should we say?
Even with our faith that believes, they sometimes still straight:
We won't band together and speak up, even if we could;
Just take a back seat, you're Inferior, I thought you understood:
We dance, sing, rap;
We have multiple skills, yet our sons and daughters
are still being killed:
Peaceful protest, Town meetings, writing letters for a solution;
Hatred, more murders, no justice is there a conclusion:
In the neighborhood OUR children are being neglected;
Under educated at school, they become disconnected:
Drinking and doing drugs,
while some of us are trying to take a stand;
We've already proved ourselves divided to THE WHITE MAN:
We walk around in a daze always on some type of high;
When the cops see us, they're already trained-that we're N.H.I
As-long-as we are killing each other, we don't see nothing wrong;

But when our children's lives are taken by a policeman,
we go to singing a sad song:
Now there's a group of ignorant people, -
Do you know what they're teaching their children;
How to be dominant through racism to prove they're Superior:
Wake up, wake up, wake up! my people before it's too late;
Before you end up dead, or someone's cell mate:
Leave your children a legacy, something to look forward to;
Don't burden them with shame, and debts from burying you:
Each and every one of us, are responsible
for turning this situation around:
We must get out of our comfort zone for it to go down:
It starts with self-respect, and then self-control;
Stop being egotistic and materialistic and
break the white man's hold:
We had a black president, but while he was in office,
society spit in his face;
With a constant reminder, it's all about race:
The prejudice evolved from state to state
killing innocent black men;
the violence didn't stop, even when the government stepped in:
The world watched live footage showing actual events;
But when it went to trial the judge was forced to acquit:
When is it going to stop, will it ever end?
These people are savages, they don't comprehend:
Some people think if they don't get involved,
it will eventually go away;
But without intervention, it's escalating and here to stay!
I'm just one of many voices, that needs to be heard;
But if we all speak together they'll become scared:
We need to stop buying all their products, and making them rich;
They'll end up depressed, without a cent:
They need us! we're part of their survival;
And we need them as well, but not as our rivals:
We must put aside our differences and form allegiance together;
Preserving life at all costs, is what really matters:

Forgiveness...

When you hold a grudge in your heart;
The pain will never part;
Your thoughts will be weighed, with a heavy load;
It's an awful burden for one to hold:
You're bottled up with tension and despair;
Convincing the world that you don't really care:
Somethings you go through, keep you worked up and pissed;
Making it close to impossible, to forgive or forget:
Now your days are cloudy, and your judgment too;
Cause you wasn't exactly sure, of what to do:
You can't hold a grudge, for as long as you live;
You must find peace with the situation, and start to forgive:
It'll relieve your mind, from all of the tension;
And pasT situations you won't have to mention:
You won't be bottled up with vengeance inside;
If you learn to forgive and swallow your pride:
Forgiveness is for you to release all the hate;
You'll begin to have peace, with less on your plate:
Nobody's perfect, we all make mistakes;
"So please forgive me, before it's too late!"

Obey...

Children of all ages obey your parents;
They have your best interest at heart, and that's for certain:
Ephesians 6:1 Children obey your parents in the Lord,
for this is right;
Your parents are here to guide you to Jesus light:
Proverbs 22:6 Train up a child in the way he should go, and when
he is older he should not depart from it.
Parents discipline your children show them spiritual guidance
if they rebel, you must insist:
Exodus 20:12 Honor your mother and your father, that your days
may be long upon the land which the Lord your God gives you.
Parents pray together as a family, and
trust in God to see you through:
Colossians 3:20 children obey your parents in everything,
for this pleases the Lord.
Parents teach your children to be loyal, to stay inspired, and
to work hard:
Matthew 19:14 but Jesus said suffer little children forbid them not,
to come on to me; for of such is the kingdom of heaven.
Parents Fast with your children, teach them to sacrifice before the
Lord by eating bread that's unleavened:
Proverbs 22:15 Folly is bound up in the heart of a child, but
the rod of discipline will drive it away.
For strength ,and repentance to God you must pray:

Parent's teach your children to be productive and responsible;
Nurture them through spiritual growth, so they'll also become accountable:
1 Corinthians 16:14 Let all that you do, be done in love.
Bring the children to church so their lives may be enriched by Our Father above:
Children listen and learn from your parents, and take their advice;
Parents through God's grace, you won't have to tell them more than twice:
Children your parents understand the things that you're going through, so don't be surprised;
They have knowledge through experiences, that's what makes them wise:
Children the bible teaches you to honor your mother and your father;
Parents pray that you're filled with the Holy Ghost Power:
So, children always do what your parents ask you to do;
God is love, your strength in Jesus shall renew:

Cocaine rule - the hell you say!!!

Cocaine is a substance that's Wicket to all;
If you even try it, be prepared to fall:
Don't convince yourself that it's just the high for joy;
Because when you come down, you're left for problems
you can't avoid;
It's always there like a black cat in the night;
The evil will try to possess you with all its might: It temps us all
young, rich, poor or old;
After you give in, it would destroy your soul:
If you don't have faith in God the Omen will stay with you;
Like a cancer without a care, regardless of what you do:
God can help remove all bad things from our sight;
Through of Prayer it will be alright:
If you can't find hope, and just another dope fiend;
Then except God in your heart he changes things:
If you continue to use it your brain will die;
And cocaine we'll have control of you, and that's no lie:
It allows you to function any kind of way;
Only to be with you, each, and every day:
You'll forget all responsibilities, and sense of time;
When you use the drug, it captivates your mind:
You're the 'World's Greatest Pretender' without problems of fear
you have no worries when crack is near:
When the drug is gone and your money runs out;
Depression sets in as you wonder about:

You'll do anything to let crack back in;
You'll lie to your mother, or steal from a friend:
If you have a family they won't matter anymore;
For having them around would just be a bore:
The effort they spend, would just be a waste, cause you and
cocaine need your own personal space:
You'll feel a strange sense of power from a $20 hit that last a
fraction of an hour;
When is gone you start to feel anxious, and inferior so you go get
some more to feel superior:
You could never get enough to feel content;
But there's satisfaction through Jesus if you only repent:
Smoking crack cocaine is a deadly sin;
Your destiny is hell, and Satan will win:
If you need help because you're hooked on that stuff; then go-to
God for an answer you can trust:
Dedicated to my brother from: heart- to- heart;

Chapter 4

Informative

1. Lead on
2. The gift
3. I see you
4. If
5. Save yourself
6. Children
7. If I must
8. Resilience
9. Time
10. The Journey
11. Race
12. Just passing through
13. Sex games
14. Loyalty
15. Now, now, now
16. Strang-er

POETRY WITH A TWIST

Lead on...

The whole country was on their knees, praying for a someone
to lead us over the hump;
We rose as-a-whole, and voted for President elect Donald Trump:
Now we've stuck with this man 4 years to come;
Knowing it out heart, that he's not the one:
His campaign strategies were all for himself;
They were meant to serve white supremacist, and no one else:
His plans to build a wall to keep the immigrants out;
Well this country was built on foreign blood, and that's no doubt:
There's no greater or lesser evil, we're all the same;
We're multicultural full of diversity, that's our name:
Drastic measures haven't worked so far;
He's trying to send us back to the 18 hundred, with a Civil War:
We can't just stand still and let him execute these plans;
He's liable to self-destruct right here on American land:
This is our country for our families to grow, flourish, and to live in;
To work, and prosper, and have a free will:
All this Prejudice and violence must stop;
Not only is it the KKK, is also from the cops:
What law's will he enforce while in that office?
How to send all men of color 2 their coffins:
A gun law was passed where all men could wear holsters,
with guns above their vest;
They'll be walking around in broad daylight
looking like the Wild, Wild, West:

What is this a movie? or just a horrible dream;
Are we living through the past? 'or trapped
in one of Hollywood's bad scenes?
This is our lives, our very own existence;
We must protest together, and be persistent:
If there was a time- it would be now -to stand up and fight;
For equality and justice for all human rights:
Now I need help enforcing this message;
For all generations to come-have the 'Rites of passage':
We can get this done, if we stick together;
And prove our loyalty, for something that really matters:
Now it's close to Donald Trump's inauguration;
We as a people we must oppose most of his conversation:
I hope you don't find this as a great big shock;
But that man is crooked, sure as the clock tick- tock:
We need some help with this mess we've jam ourselves in;
He's talking about messing with the foreign trade,
I don't see a win;
These countries are our allies, and they also have our back;
Hell- they own half of United States, and
we can't even afford to buy it back:
Let's use our common sense, and be realistic;
Before we all end up losing, and become a statistic:

The Gift...

It's a woman going around;
Spreading poems throughout the town;
Exposing truth, and stating facts;
Telling people about themselves:
God blessed her with insight;
To tell a story and tell it right:
She's bringing joy and a bit of cheer;
Though all the messages that you hear:
When you sit down to listen;
It makes you aware of what you're missing:
She has a special type of gift;
When you hear-your life will shift:
I don't believe it's actually, planned;
Because she writes poems on demand:
She'll tell you if you mean or nice;
She'll write it once and read twice:
There's no need for attitude;
Her poems will surely change your mood:
She'll make you think and realize;
Respect truth, and not the lies:
The words are coming from her soul;
She's very wise and in control:
She's writes doing the day and during the night;
And when she's done, it's a big delight:
I'm very glad I heard her work;

When I started to laugh, it made her smirk:
If you haven't heard her yet;
You're in for a treat, and that's a fact:
She has a lot of confident;
She'll make you cry, she'll make you vent:
She's always willing to share her gift;
Making sure your mind doesn't drift:
She's has a lot of information;
To leave you with some inspiration:
So, come on over listen-up;
The words she got will fill you up:
If I said it once, I'll say it twice;
The poems she writes are very nice:
I never heard nothing so unique before;
It's makes you want more, and more!

I See You...

I write for my heart, I give it my all;
Some of my listeners resist, and build up a wall:
You know when I'm writing, and talking about you;
You try to hide your emotions, but I see right through:
I'm not trying to be cocky, or arrogant;
But I'm very confident, and sure of it:
When a poet gets ahold of you, there's nowhere to run;
He'll expose you with words, as if you've been shun:
Be careful what you think, cause I can see that too;
Your thoughts are not your own, just the words are new:
I'm your mirror, not your looking glass;
What you refuse to see, without the mask:
It's not always entertaining, sometimes it hurts;
With the truth in front of you, you're on high alert:
I'm giving you my advice, take my words with stride;
Just be attentive and swallow your pride:
Life is not always about cause, and effect;
Sometimes it's about the simple things, you neglect:
You know when it's wrong, after you evaluate;
But you settle for substitutes, to compensate:
When things are not really meeting your standards of perfection;
You hide behind a LIE, and try to protect it:
I see you, rather you want me to or not;
I'm your conscience, calling you out:

If...

If there was no light to see by;
will it be darkness?
if there were no rain clouds;
will it be a drought?
if there was no land;
could we do without?
if it wasn't for the wind;
will there be a breeze?
if the trees didn't grow;
will they not bear fruit or leaves?
if the ocean didn't rise;
would there be a tide?
if the air wasn't clean;
could we breathe outside? .
if it wasn't for men;
would animal rule the world?
if it wasn't for a woman;
will there be no boy or girl?
if the sun didn't shine;
would there be no fire or heat?
if the gas poison the world;
will there be food to eat?

Save yourself...

You want me to write what's real?
Then I need to write what I feel:
On our knees we need to bow;
For the King we won't allow;
To fill our hearts and our homes,
With his Holy Ghost Power:
Ain't none of us getting out of here alive;
The question is do we choose to live or survive?
While you're out there hustling trying to make ends meet;
Putting the next brother or sister beneath your feet:
But you're doing right by yours, or at least that's what
you tell yourself in order to sleep:
So you gave up your dream, and you rub it in your kid's face;
How you sacrifice to put food on the table, and
clothes on their back:
And they better show you some respect, and stay in a child's place:
Where is their place?
But you don't even respect yourself;
You're an example by feeding your body, but not the soul;
They have no choice, but to be lost, they're not even whole:
Their whole existence is a lie;
You said "God said to be fruitful and multiply":
Now you want to take a text from the bible, as if
it's some kind of game;
Take the children to Our Father, and teach them his name:

They're not your children, they're loaned to you;
It's up to you to have the courage, to bring them back to Jesus,
it's the right thing to do:
You got a demonic forces out here
pulling you in all different directions;
That's because you're not grounded, under Jesus protection:
Why you're out here stalling and trying to buy you some time;
The devil got you so confuse, you can't make up your mind:
Now, you cry yourself to sleep, cause you're in a whole lot of pain;
Using drugs and drinking, about to go insane:
You look up to heaven saying "Lord why me", as-you use
his name in vein:
The devil starts talking "I'mma kill myself, I'm gonna
do it right here"!
"It won't even matter, don't nobody care"!
Just one last selfish act for the road;
And devil's waiting-you've already sold your soul:
It's not over, just because you end your life;
You're going straight to HELL, to become the devil's wife:
You think Jesus died for all of this hassle;
If he didn't intend to put his people in a castle:
I don't know about you, but I'm following the path of
righteousness, to the road that leads to the Gate;
There's no split decision, there's no debate:
I refused to deny my Lord, while I'm alive;
I choose to be faithful and live eternally,
not to kill the God inside of me, just to survive:
When you get past all the violence, the crimes, the racism,
and the hate:
You left with a 'Soul' decision, that you need to make:
You wanna blame it on the next, instead of owning your own;
Staying on a pity pot, singing the same 'sad song';
God ain't looking for the weak, his building up the strong:
They'll understand Joy coming in the morning,
after their suffering may be long:
He's choosing soldiers to fight in the army for the Lord:
Surrendering to his will is your first start:

We're constantly at war, and everything's a test;
And you're not the only one going through something,
we all need to confess:
It's not about the money, the car you drive, or
how well you can dress;
It's about winning Souls, and saving Souls, to be blessed:
I need to stress this point, and sync it in;
I don't think you clearly understand what it means,
to devour your temple, with lust and sin:
While you're chasing behind people, looking for comfort, saying
they're just a friend;
God see's all, and he knows all, he knew the outcome,
before it began:
That's doesn't mean, continue drown the same path, and
allow Satan to win:
He's a God of mercy, and second chance;
All you have to do, is ask him for forgiveness, when
you put together your hands:
He gave us all free will, to make our own choice;
It's up to us to give God the glory as we left our voice:
Out of a man's mouth is his heart;
So you say things that sounds good, as if you're being smart;
You think if you're educated, you'll be doing your part:
God is the only judge, there's no court:
This is probation, right here on earth, so you need to get it right;
And decide on who's war, you're going to fight:
We're in a spiritual warfare, and it's constantly on move;
For Heaven sake people, give your life to Jesus,
the rapture is coming soon:
No man knows the day or the hour;
You need to be prayed up, packed up, and ready to be picked up,
filled up with the Holy Ghost Power:
Stop sitting around thinking it's all about you;
God needs all of our souls as a whole to see this though:
Save yourself and I'll save me as well;
Then we'll sing together to the Lord, with something to tell:

For all these preachers, talking about planting a seed;
Making them rich, ain't doing God no good deed:
You can't buy your way to Heaven, it ain't for sale:
Jesus paid in full, when he was crucified, and
hung up by rusty nails:
The true sacrifice is when you give your life to Jesus, and
you give up your time;
Stop giving in-to will of the enemy and peace you'll find:
I know I've giving you a whole lot to swallow, and
it all has to soak in;
If you don't remember nothing else, ask God for forgiveness,
repent right now, and let Jesus in:

Children...

Children- you have them, so you can have a little part of yourself;
Little did you know, they were going to move out, and
take the rest:
When they're born the first thing you say is,
"Oh how cute and sweet";
Until you get that bill, from all the food they need to eat:
We work all day to care of our family, and home;
Even hire a sitter, so they don't be left alone:
You go into debt, trying to live the 'Family 'dream;
30 years later, you just want to scream:
We spoil them, and love them, and praised their work;
And they grew up to be brats, and sometimes jerks:
You take them to nice places, and buy them nice things;
You treat them as if they were royal Kings and Queens:
When you refuse to give them the things, that they want;
They throw tantrums, and do things to break your heart:
The only rules you have, is for them is to do their chores;
They scream in your face, saying
they don't want to live there no more!
You give them a good education, so they are grow up and be smart;
So, one day they'll move out and do their part:
The cycle continues, when they have kids of their own;
They would've made different choices, if they only known:

If I Must...

Some of my poems appear to be harsh,
I'm not trying to be mean;
When people hear the truth they just want to scream:
Do I just stop writing to satisfy them?
Or do I just write what they want to hear?
Right this minute I'm at a loss of words;
Because some people got hurt by the things they heard:
I thought it was about being brutally honest;
But if I don't lie and make them feel good, then
they don't want to hear nothing:
Who am I to judge them? Who am I- if not me?
I just write what I feel and I write what I see!
You think it's easy for me to just whip up word or 2?
No, I actually, considered how it affects you:
If I knew it-but didn't tell it, you'll keep up a fuss;
So, it'll be as I write- if I must:
Some poems are meant to be informative;
Some expose the way we live:
Some make us laugh, some make us cry;
Other's tell our story after we die!
It's sometimes hard to do, or say the right things;
But when you know it's true, just accept what I bring:
I won't alter my words to accommodate you;
You don't get nothing for the message if you can't hear the truth:

JACQUELINE JAMES

Someone needs to tell it, so why not let it be me;
I'll be gentle as possible and tell it humbly:
I'll make sure it's accurate and that you can trust;
I'll write both the good and the bad- if I must:
Just stay with me now, just hear me out;
I'll teach you to listen I'll show you how:
You'll find some inner peace, what everyone's talking about;
When you face them dark secrets, that I write about:
Don't get upset, I don't even know your name;
It could be my truths, we're all the same:
I don't what to hear you yell, I don't want to hear you cuss;
I just want to write my thoughts- if I must:
I was once told- "don't share that! you need to keep to yourself;"
But if I kept everything you didn't want to hear- to myself;
There'll be nothing to write about, there'll be nothing left:
I'm still undecided everything that needs to be said;
So, I'm going to put this poem the rest, and go to bed:

Resilience...

I am the epiphany of resilience;
After being molested, rape, and abuse;
Through God's grace, I'm able to share the news:
I've spent my life giving to others, even when they decide to take;
Now it's my time to shine, and no sound shall they make:
I've conquered challenges, beyond your wildest imagination;
Yet, I survived and was too able to fulfill my obligations:
I've come a long way, and many obstacles I've overcome;
I started new traditions, and I beat by my own drum:
God has spared me humiliations;
During my silent times of desperation:
My life is complex, and very unique;
I stay humble, but I'm no- where- near weak:
My focus is only on things that matters the most;
My relationship with Jesus, my family, and a few other folks:
I hope everyone appreciates the simple things I've done;
The love I've giving, and the hearts I've won:
I would like to share a little bit of my style;
Praying that one day God will say "Well done my Fairchild"!:

Time...

We have little, no more, or less than we need;
We try to extend our limits, cause of our geed:
It's here for now, but gone in a blink;
As the time goes on, we value it more, I think:
It's precious to all and can never be replaced;
It's priceless to everyone, of every creed, and race:
It can't be duplicated, it's only here for one time;
The thoughts of its presence, is only caught in your mind:
Sometimes it comes, and we wished it never exist;
Other times we demand more, and even persist:
We come into a new place we haven't been yet-today;
Only through time, are we allowed to stay:
Once it's gone, it's over, never to be returned again;
It won't wait, or stand still, even though it's our friend:
Sometimes it's on your side, and sometimes it's just not;
So if you're not playing attention, it won't wait, or stop:
"Please can I have a moment of your time, just a second or two?"
"So that I can convince you of a thought, that'll be right for you!"
Time -we waste it, we loan it, it's not ours to give;
It's only here for a moment, in order to live:
With bad choices, we get caught up in places we don't want to be;
Those are times we regret, until we're eventually set free;
Take your time and be careful to do things right;
It's your time if you spend it, partying all night:

Sometimes are good, and other times are bad;
Sometimes we're excited, and other's we're sad:
Sometimes there's things that we often neglect;
And other times we treasure, and never forget:
So never let a minute, or second go by;
Use your time wisely, even if you just have to cry:
We hold fast to its joy, and dismiss it's sorrows:
Cause it's here today, and gone tomorrow:

The Journey...

We journey through life to find ourselves, and what we made of;
I know who I am, I'm comfortable in my skin, and that I love:
Sometimes it's hard to understand what you -need- from you;
You serve others, still confused on what you need to do:
We attend motivational seminars, we read self-help books;
The answers right in front of you, just take a look:
Some of us work 9 to 5 /7 to 3 / 8 to 4;
We come home from work satisfied, thinking there's nothing more:
As long as we can pay our bills, keep a roof over my head, and food on the table;
As long as it's honest work, a steady job, we don't mind the labor:
The travel is all planned, but the destiny is unknown;
The path we take, will be our own:
We undermined ourselves in most cases;
We don't trust our instinct, to take us to higher places:
The majority of our life, we're puzzled and lost;
Wanting to be a followers, instead of the boss:
Some people did this- and- that, and they got ahead;
Okay, but make your own route count for you, instead:
The answer may not come in an instant;
We have to take the journey, and go to distance:
You're on the other side of the road, waiting to meet you;
Seeing what you made of, and what you're qualified to do:
Give yourself some time- "to yourself be true";

Fall in love with you, I'm sure it's going to be new:
You'll be surprised how much you have in common, with You!;
I guarantee you if you take a chance, you'll understand just what to do:
Your route is not mine- nor mine is yours;
Our paths may be different, but we both want reward:
Sometimes we get off track and start looking for self-gratification;
But you'll find satisfaction though a spiritual relation:
Our creator is waiting on the other side;
Master of the universe his name is God!!!!.........

Race...

My ethnicity, and race is all confused;
The society speak of us to bring bad news:
We're already stereotyped, as being the worst of the worst;
I was cursed by the plague, right from birth:
I really don't know my nationality, I'm mixed with some of this,
and some of that;
I'm more than African-American, and that's a fact:
My skin is caramel, it's beautiful to me;
There's nothing you can say, to lower my self-esteem:
We shouldn't be judged by race, or the color of our skin;
What defines a man, is his character to within:
The Americans are not our true friends;
And in the African race, we don't fit in:
African-American, what is exactly does that mean?
A race of people spawn, from the white man's sin:
We were rejected from the very start;
And, label as being ignorant, and a bunch of retards:
We were given common names, that follows us throughout our life;
Hoping to gain heritage, when a man takes a wife:
All the generations to come, will bear that name.
Not knowing the circumstances, or understanding the shame:
We just continue on trying to live an everyday life;
Until their prejudiced hit's us, and we're in for a fight:

We had to fight for freedom, we had to fight for equality,
we have to fight for justice;
We have to fight for civil rights, we have to fight for equal rights,
we have to fight for human rights:
Haven't our ancestors fought enough to pay the price
for all our life's?
I'm tired of fighting- I don't know about you;
The struggle is long, and the fight isn't though:
We all need to keep our armor of protection;
God's grace will lead us in the right direction:
No matter what our ethnicity, race, creed, or color;
Through God's eyes we are all sisters and brothers:
So, next time you look at the skin on my face;
Remember to judge me by my heart, and not my RACE:..

Just passing through…

You looked-into my eyes and saw my soul;
Out of my mouth unspeakable secrets from my past,
immediately start to unfold:
I couldn't control the urge to confess, as if my days depended on
you knowing all my truths, or was it just a test?
I felt compelled to tell you everything relevant or not;
Some necessary and some you didn't even need to know about:
Now I'm stuck waiting wondering, are you my judge and jury too?
Hoping for your acceptance needing your approval,
wishing you understood;
Why I'm just passing through:
You caught my attention and that's sometimes hard to do;
Now we're trapped in a bubble, with all eyes on me and you:
Things that seem to be important, may not really be at all;
Showing false pride can make us all rise, and fall:
Nothing is never what it appears to be;
So, let's just take our time to grow, learn, listen, and see:
When we're together I enjoy each moment with you;
If only I could freeze time, and didn't realize,
I was just passing through:
Wanting something, is not the same as being free to express it;
Giving something, it's not the same as being able to accept it:
Appreciation is when you reach that level of control;
In your hands, or your actions, your future, and destiny to be hold:

I found a place of contentment from the peace in your voice;
Allowing things to grow to greater heights, was my own choice:
I'll cherish our love, cause it's so sweet and new;
And pray it last forever- while I'm just passing through:

Sex Games…

Sex talk can you comprehend, the rules of the game;
Now will you ever win?
The power of the word, that's what I mean;
Body language goes to the extreme:
Sexy signals is where it all begins;
Lustful thoughts and friendly-friend:
The way you wear those tight clothes, you should watch out;
Because they're saying it's playtime, without a doubt:
So watch your moves, before you have a sex relation;
It may not really meet, your expectations:
There's an old way, is called friendly sex talk;
Is someone that's expresses dirty words, then
tell them to take a walk:
Don't try to choose all in one night;
Avoid the freaks, and make it right:
Search around and try to find the best;
If they're too outgoing, don't get caught up in that mess:
You need morals and respect to qualify;
To have sex for love, and not a lie:
If you not really sure, of what it might cost you;
Then use a condom to take some precaution:
Read here and there, to become educated;
Because today's sex, is very complicated:

So understand if you will;
Simple communication, is your brightest skill:
Find a technique to negotiate;
Identify the style of your associate:
If it seems understanding, and you agreed that is fair;
With a little bit of guidance, then sex you'll share:
Just don't be misled, and make sex your profession;
As a commodity, it'll teach you a lesson:
It makes no difference if you young, or old;
Bad sex is something, that threatens the soul:
Don't have sex because there's nothing else to do;
Or just because they said 'They'll marry you':
Unwanted children, is what you'll be minding;
If you have sex when it's really bad timing:
Adult fantasies is surely okay;
But don't be fooled, that all sex is that way:
If you're young, and need some help;
Consult an elder, take the first step:
Why have sex, if it's premature;
Appreciation is when you're sure:
Growing is about learning, and living;
Is not about, all that sex you're giving:
Saying "No", is your best weapons;
If you're still just an adolescent:
For you older ones, who influences the kids;
You ought to know, that's nothing but sin:
Before you go ahead, and break the ice;
Please my friend, experience life:
The universe is a definite key;
Which relates to both you and me:
Cosmic flows goes here and there;
It affects us all, when sex is near:
Explore the world, take first- things- first;
Be selective, before you settle for worse:
There'll always going be at least one mistake;
But with common sense, the 'Bull' you won't take:

Confrontation, and criticism is usually healthy, in
making a good decision:
Don't give in, and show you're weak;
If you do, bad sex will have you beat:
Talking and doing is two different things;
Don't give in, until have that ring:
Marriage is the only vow;
That separates us all, that God allows:;
Sex with lovers or just a friend;
We all should think twice, before allowing them in:
They come in your soul, not joint as one;
Then soon sex to them, is just some fun:
Us as parents, should heed the rules;
That sex, is something we all must school:
To our children, we need to tell them, that they must learn;
To have sex 'my dear' you must wait your turn:
Grateful hints from me-to-you...
And hope your sex-wise, when I'm through:
True confession is your real protection;
When you're going to release a sex connection!

Loyalty...

Where does your loyalty lye?
With your old friends you've known for a while;
Or new pals, that supports your style:
Is it with the ones who clearly have your back;
Are they just there, when you need someone to pick up the slack:
Is it with your family members, because you don't have a choice;
Are you just a coward, who refuses to use your voice:
Is it with the ones who house's you, clothed you, and
give you-your next meal;
Or with the ones you party with at night, and
give you a cheap thrill:
Where does you loyalty lye?
With your companion, your spouse or your significant other;
How about your absent father, or dedicated mother:
How about your nosy neighbor, who watches your house
while you're on vacation;
What about the school administration, who helps your children
with their education:
Maybe it's with your pledges, doing your old college days;
Perhaps it's with your daily acquaintances, who's
always giving you your way:
How about your play sister, your God sister, or your best friend;
What about the one you'll share your money with,
when you have it spend:

Ok, is it with your partner, your buddy, or
your brother from another mother;
How about your homie, your gang members, or
your actual brother:
Where does your loyalty lye?
What about your classmates, your roommates, or
even your first dates;
Is it with your daddy, your step daddy, or all the losers you hate:
Is it with your coworkers, your supervisor, or your colleagues;
Maybe it's with your boss, who
gives you raises to meet your needs:
How about your mortgage broker, your realtor, or your landlord;
Is it with the ones who praises you, and
give you recognition after you've worked hard:
How about your children, step children, or people you take care of;
How about your parents, your elders, and
the ones you claim you love:
Is it with your grandparents, your uncles or your aunts;
Or is it with your favorite person, who you truly love a lot:
Perhaps your groupies, your followers, or
the ones in your social click;
Is it with your cousins, who think they're street hustlers, and
always trying to be slick:
How about your priest, your bishop, or
minister trying to enrich your life;
Or is it with your church members who say they're
your sisters and brothers through Christ:
Where does your loyalty lye?
My loyalty is with Our Lord and Savior Jesus Christ;
Who gave up his life and died on the cross to pay the price:
And my loyalty is with Our Father from Above;
Who gives us Grace and Mercy through his Love:

Now, now, now...

You hurt me, you hurt me bad:
You knew I'll never fit in, and be classy;
I'll be labels a slut, and even trashy:
You hurt me, you hurt me bad;
You stole my childhood, it altered my life;
You knew I'll never be pure, to be a man's wife:
You hurt me, you hurt me bad:
You told me to be quiet, don't tell, just hush;
But I've kept your secret long enough;
You hurt me, you hurt me bad:
I tried to bring you my friends, and random girls;
You refused to touch them, or change their world:
You hurt me; you hurt me bad:
You took away my first love, when you took away my choice;
I had no sounds to make, when you took away my voice:
You hurt me, you hurt me bad;
I've lived with the shame, and guilt for too long;
I thought by holding it in, it kept me strong:
You hurt me, you hurt me bad:
I need to release this pain, speak the words in the wind;
So, I can be free, and learn to live without sin:
You hurt me, you hurt me bad:

Jacqueline James

You took away my innocence, you used me over and over again,
and when you were done, you gave me to your friends:
You hurt me, you hurt me bad:
I never understood why I became so promiscuous;
Why no decent man, would make me his Mrs.:
You hurt me, you hurt me bad:
You had plenty of choices, but you kept coming for me;
I was a child, I thought it was love;
I couldn't clearly see:
You hurt me, you hurt me bad:
You went on and became very successful, and proud;
While I laid dormant, scared to speak in a crowd:
You hurt me, you hurt me bad:
I didn't even want to know, but now I know why- why I stayed sad
all the time, but wasn't able to cry:
You hurt me, you hurt me bad:
I convinced myself, that you never knew what you were doing;
Until you told me 40 years later, about a girl you refuse to ruin:
You hurt me, you hurt me bad:
I can read this out loud, I never call your name;
But you know who you are;
You're the one I blame:
You hurt me, you hurt me bad:
Years ago, I used alcohol and drugs, to drown my sorrows;
God took it away, and gave me brighter tomorrow's
You hurt me, you hurt me bad:
It was still a lot of pain, I was holding inside;
I needed to forgive you for me;
I could no longer hide:
You hurt me, you hurt me bad:
But I'm letting you know today, I'm no longer sad:

Strang-er...

I saw a stranger passing by;
With a blink-of-an-eye, I wanted to cry:
For that split second, she caught my attention;
I heard her heartbeat, when I decided to listen:
Her thoughts were all fuzzy, I could hardly hear;
She was really fragile, I could smell her fear:
She wanted to scream, as she turned around;.
But she felt my presence, and made no sound:
I didn't disturb her, it wasn't my place;
The distraught in her eyes, gleamed on her face:
The moment that passed, seem to be hours;
I denied her myself, was I just a coward?
I had nothing to offer, other than empathy;
But at the time, I wasn't good company:
I tried to speak when I pulled it together;
But she was long- gone, like my breath in the weather:

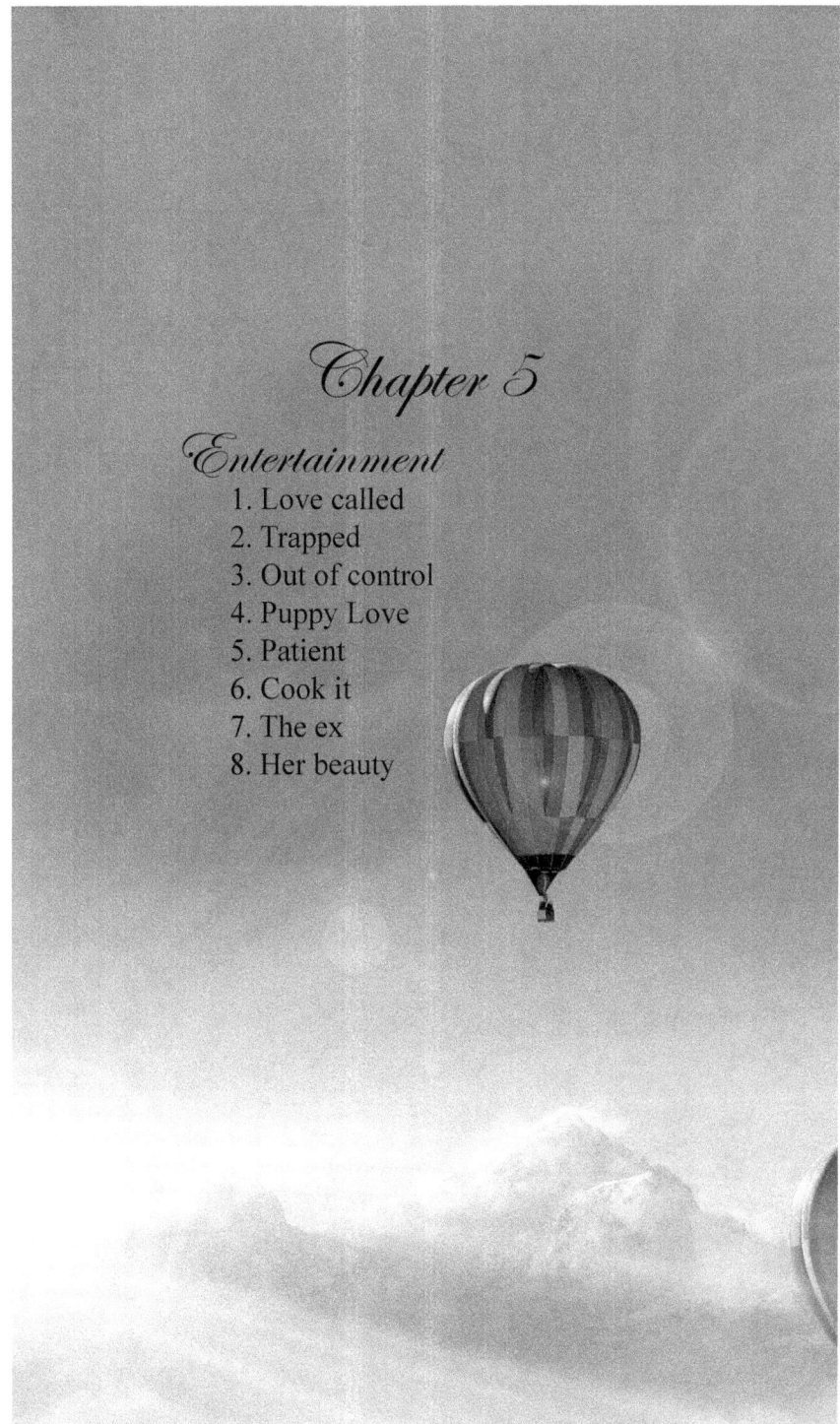

Chapter 5
Entertainment
1. Love called
2. Trapped
3. Out of control
4. Puppy Love
5. Patient
6. Cook it
7. The ex
8. Her beauty

POETRY WITH A TWIST

Love called...

I can sail across the ocean, I can admire the sea;
As I sit back and long, for the love you once had for me:
Your lips was once filled with wonder and surprise;
When they filtered through the night, to meet my light brown eyes:
Untangling though tangible storms;
Only to find refuge, in my lustful arms;
There's hasn't been another, to love me that way;
While I'm stampeding, like wild horses to this day:
I didn't appreciate you, when you were here;
Yet, I have the nerve to ask "Can you please come back dear"
I know in my heart, our reality will never be the same;
Because I put you through unnecessary crap, I embarrassed you,
and caused you pain:
I build-up all the scars, on my own and for that I'm ashamed:
However, I still hold my pillow at night, and call out your name:
To touch the silk from my skin;
Like the petals of a rose, it has to grow to begin:
All the things we did, and all of the things that were said;
Has no merits, if they're only in my head:
I know I messed up, and you've probably moved up;
But the ocean rose high in my heart, as I sing my sad song:
Your touch was soothing, to calm the salvage beast;
But my raging spirit, didn't allow Love to conquer and defeat;

If I do it all again differently, it'll still would remain the same;
With the charm of a Prince, and strength of a rocket soaring
to the stars, you couldn't tame, my name:
So memories are mine to hold;
In your arms I once was, now I'm here to bear my soul:
Empty as a closet, in a cobweb filled attic;
With no class you're scorned, and I'm hopelessly pathetic:
Romance to no degree, shall I find;
When love called-no answer, now it's no longer mine:

Trapped...

Trapped within my own walls of solitude;
Speaking a language, only I can understand;
My desperate cry for redemption, goes unanswered:
Screaming, ranting, and trying to break free, from this prison in
which I've so conveniently engage my thoughts in;
My pathetic need to be heard, is superficial;
Skepticism progress as I've become more hesitant to unlock the
door, that will surely free me for my own misery;
I've convinced myself of a strategy,
that will persuade me to use the key;
What.... There's a key?
How awfully predictable I've become:

Out of Control...

Lord don't stop me;
The devil can't block me:
I'm on a roll; I'm out of control, just writing real bold:
And my poems are cold:
I'm up all-night, cause, I like when I write;
I just talked to text, I don't need no light:
I'm trying to share with the world a little part of me;
And bring a little clarity to the things I see:
Don't try to stop me, just let me be:
I write about this, and I write about that;
I write about the truth, and I write about the facts:
I tell one story, then, I move on to the next;
If I leave out something, I'll write the rest:
I'll make you smile, I'll try my best:
So just let me write, cause I'm on a roll;
Right about now, I'm out of control:

Puppy love…

Four month old, weighting 98 pounds;
5'8" on your hinds, bout to knock me down:
And you're just a puppy, you're not even grown;
But you're so beautiful, I had to bring you home:
You still had baby teeth, you couldn't even chew a bone;
You get your canines in your mouth when you're grown:
You were so sweet, and adorable;
Just watching you play was so enjoyable:
You're all white, pure as the driven snow;
I glad your previous owners, let you go:
God could've made a more beautiful animal;
All the tricks you know, you should've been in a carnival:
When I sit on the couch, you jump in my lap;
You try to lay real still, and take you a nap:
You're so cute, and lovable too;
But you're too big for a lap dog, that's for sure:
You're part of the family, and very spoil;
And you know you're mama's 'baby-boy':
The whole family fell in love with you, from the start;
You're so fun-loving and very smart:
You greet me at the door, stand on your hind legs, and
put your paws around my waist;
Then show me all your love, by licking me in my face:

One thing for sure you can't be confined;
You broke the door off your kennel, and
you jumped out the window:
I put you in the bathroom for the maintenance men;
But you chewed a hole through the wall, and came on in:
I had a privacy fence built so you couldn't jump out;
You just knock that down, and still ran about:
I had you in the back yard, chained to a tree;
But you snapped the chain in half, and came running to me:
I put you in a room downstairs and closed the door;
But you came right back up, you escaped though floor:
I take you for long walks, to stretch your legs;
When we get back home you want to jump in my bed:
I put you in the car to go for a ride;
You lean halfway out the window, to stare outside:
I take you to the park to run around;
When we get back home, you're ready to lay down:
So I left you alone, and let you be;
Now you follow me around, to see what I see:
You go get your toys, when you're ready to play;
And you enjoy yourself, having a doggy-dog day:

Patient...

Hurry, hurry, hurry up, and wait;
I'm moving fast, cause I'm running late:
Patience is a virtue in everything we say and do;
If you don't slow down, it might just hinder you:
If you speak too fast, you thoughts might clash;
And you'll in up talking trash:
Good things come to those who wait;
And we'll learn how to appreciate:
Please wait-wait your turn;
A bit of humbleness, you will earn:
If you go to fast, and rush right through;
You'll never learn, just what to do:
Please slow down, and just relax;
Give yourself a moment, to catch your breath:
There may be storms raging in your life, that needs to pass;
It's just a test from God, that will not last:
When disappointments come, and we don't get upset;
We express patients, and that's truly blessed:
Managing your behavior in a positive way;
Is exercising self-control throughout your day:
When facing trouble or even delay;
Patience gives us the capacity to accept it, when we pray:
When you wait patiently, God will give you peace;
And you'll find your burdens, have all been relieved:
So be slow to respond, and just be still:
God is watching you, for a blessing to give:

Cook it...

What's cooking, good-looking?, that's what they all ask;
I cook up a bunch of good food, then I relax:
I cook steaks, pasta, and 'soul food', too;
I create authentic recipe, that's what I do:
Cooking is my passion, and I have lots of fun;
I'll invite you to eat with me, and I hope you come:
I cook spaghetti, macaroni, and all types of rice;
I cook with perfection, and serve it up nice:
I use special ingredients, in my vegetarian soup;
They're freshly prepared, and the recipes are new:
I cook carrots, broccoli, and cauliflower;
I'll cook all fresh vegetables, within the hour:
I cook fried chicken, baked chicken, and honey barbecue as well:
I cook it with love, and it turns out swell:
I cook lots of proteins, even beans with ham hocks;
You'll get your nutrients, and you'll get a lot:
I cook fried wings, buffalo wings, and hot wings;
I cook pizzas, French fries, and all sorts of things:
I cook all the foods that you chose to eat;
I'll cook it all, with or without meat:
I cook Chinese, Italian, and Mexican;
I trek their recipes, cause I can:
If you want something different, or totally new:
Whatever you're craving, I'll cook it up for you:
I cook burritos, fajitas, and tacos;

JACQUELINE JAMES

I put in chicken, beef, cheese, and whatever goes:
I cook chuck roast, round roast, and pork shoulder roast;
I'll serve it with mashed potatoes, or a baked potatoes, and Texas toast:
You'll eat everything on your plate, just like you should;
Then come back for seconds, I knew you would:
I make garlic bread, cheese bread, and wheat buttered bread;
I'll make sure your stomach's full, when you get feed:
I cook cat fish, cod fish, and buffalo;
And I insist that you taste them all, before you go:
If you're Vegan, and don't eat meat, then I got you covered as well;
I'll cook a spicy bean casserole hold the meat and the Mayo:
I cook a bean burrito wrapped in a wheat tortilla shell, with a homemade sauce;
It tastes so authentic, you'll call it 'the boss':
I make a special layer salad, no eggs, no dressing;
You have to try it, you don't know what you're missing:
I cook fried shrimp, garlic butter sautéed shrimp, and steamed shrimp:
I serve it with cocktail sauce or a Cajun dip:
I cook neckbones with potatoes, beans with neckbones, and barbecue neckbones;
If try them all, you'll be licking your fingers, when it's gone:
I cook 7 bone steaks, cube steaks, and sirloin steak;
All cooked to perfection, I don't make no mistakes:
I cook porterhouse, filet mignon, add New York strips;
If you go to a restaurant, you'll be wasting a trip:
I cook beef liver, and rice smothered with gravy;
It be so tender and delicious, just what you're craving:
I cook pork steak, pork chops, baked or fried;
They're bursting with so much favor, you won't need no sides:
I cook chicken fettuccine, shrimp alfredo, and stuffed manicotti;
When you eat at my house, you know it's a party:
I cook lobster tails, oysters, and even crab legs;
I cook a variety of foods, that's what I said:

When you visit my home, you will eat;
I won't stop cooking, until I'm tired of standing on my feet:
I'll cook everything in the freezer, and serving up with a bun;
And we'll all eat together, when I'm done:

The Ex...

Scratching picking like a rat;
Oh, my goodness is my ex;
It's over now and that's a fact:
You didn't appreciate it when you was in;
Now you want to be my friend:
Our time has passed, so let it be;
You're the last person, I want to see:
You got your thing, so go ahead on;
I don't want you in my home:
Hang up the phone, stop calling me;
Hearing your voice, is bothering me:
I don't wanna go out with you;
You need to find you somebody new:
Get some business of your own;
I just want you to leave me alone:
There's nothing left to talk about;
It's over now, so move on out:
Listen to you-not right now;
It's a waste of time-I won't allow:
You're my ex, you're in my past;
And I'm glad that junk didn't last:
All the stuff you put me through;
And you claimed, it wasn't you;
You're going around telling lies;
How we broke up, and the reason why:

It doesn't matter anymore;
Just leave my house, and close the door:
Get out my face, get out my life;
I never wanna be your wife:
Gone now, I don't wanna be rude;
But now, I got an attitude:
I don't wanna see you on the street;
Just keep on walking, if we meet:
You need to show a little tact;
You're not my friend- you're my ex:

Her Beauty...

Rippling through the ocean tides;
Watching the Sun as it rise:
Behold her bottom filled with treasures;
Countless gems, to no measure:
Dare less surfers, wanting to ride;
The highest point, from her tide:
Swilling around as the wind grow strong:
Brightly shinning as the day is long:
Beating though the breast of the ocean's shore:
Attracting tourist, as she roars:
Navy blue is her color, at the bottom of her bed;
Topaz fills the top of her head:
Light blue, and green covers the middle of her seam:
Her belly's filled with tropical fish;
To name them all, would be your wish:
Fishermen come, and sailors go;
To watch their catch, would be a show:
Collecting oysters and seashells;
For the absent ones, please do tell:
Brightly shines the sun her way;
Freezing though, a sweaty day:
Tourist swim at her edge, they meet;
Brushing the sand, from their feet:

Hundreds of waves flutters past;
Blowing wind that cannot last:
Taking pictures when you're near;
Needed to know her beauty there:
Embracing the ocean, as your friend;
Desires to return, again and again:

Purple...

The color of purple, so majestic and loved;
Worn by Our King up above:
Growing is a beautiful field of purple lilies;
Charming with her fragrance like- a filly:
Stumpy and trapping gracefully through, for hours;
Radiating color to the flower:
Given the Sun a reason to shine;
Desiring admiration, and Divine:
Glowing through the night seen by many;
Its passion endures plenty:
Calm and soothing, yet gentle on the eyes;
Can't resist, when passing by:
Compliments the scenery, with a beautiful blend;
Smooth and relaxing-to comprehend:
Thoughts of fulfillment, heavenly sent;
Alluring with ultimate pleasure meant:
Brightness to be seen through lighter form;
Darkness draw near, when it's royal:
Violet makes its way through my heart;
Fragrance seducing, my very start:
Orchids, lilac are the flower:
Steady by calm -near the hour:
Adorable site ready to please;
Grabs behold me, I'm not to tease:
Times to be satisfied for my heart;
Spectacular color- not to part:

The Loaner...

Please return the car, it was just a loaner;
I need to take it back, to its rightful owner:
He loaned to me, and I loaned to you;
Which was a foolish thing to do;
Now he's waiting on me to bring it back;
He has no ideal, it's you I can't track:
He was being nice, and doing me a favor;
But I took him for grated, cause I was able:
Now he's calling and calling, blowing up my phone;
And I'm having people lie, saying I'm not home:
Now it's been 2 days, and I'm still waiting on you;
You're wrong for that, and you're ratchet too:
Why are you stalling, give me back the car;
It's not your property, you've gone too far:
While you're having fun, and out there rolling;
He's going to mess around and call it- in-stolen:
You're be in a whole lot of trouble, if he calls the police;
He doesn't own that car, is still under lease:
It's a company car, and it's in his boss's name;
We're all going down, and that's a shame:
Where you at man?, quit messing around;
Like you disappeared without a trace, or a sound:
All of this confusion, and I was just supposed to go to the store;
He's never going to loan me nothing else anymore:

Just think about his boss, who loaned it to him;
The company's going to FIRE both of them:
So bring back the car man, it's not your toy;
While you're riding around the city, with your boy:
While you're driving around at someone else's expense;
I'm at home hiding, biting my nails, and feeling tense:
What is it going to take, to make this right?
You're looking good, riding around in broad day light:
You're very selfish, and also bold;
The stuff you're doing, is out of control:
He trusted me, and you screwed us all;
I'm just going to tell him to make that call:
The company trusted his boss, his boss trusted him, he trusted me, and I trusted you;
Now you're telling me, that you've loaned it out too:
Get the car back NOW, that's what I mean!
This is so messed up, I NEED TO SCREAM!!!

Friends...

Some are new, others are old;
Some get in your heart, others your soul':
If we lucky we get one or more;
To call a friend, that we adore:
Some are here for a season;
Others we meet, for a reason:
Nevertheless, they always around;
Greeting you with a smile, and not a frown:
It's always good to have one or two;
To help you decide, on what to do:
If you get that one who has your back;
It's a special connection, and that's a fact:
You never have to worry about doing without;
Because they know what you need, before you open your mouth:
They laugh with you, cry with you, and party too;
And sometimes even bend the rules:
They'll borrow your things, and never pay you back;
When you ask about it, they start talking smack:
So you tolerated it, so you better get ready;
Are you'll lose your friend, over something real petty:
We trust them with our deep secrets, and most intimate desires;
We share our present, we share our priors:
We share our time, we share our cash;
We also share adventures, from our past:

Jacqueline James

We take lots of pictures, looking real cool;
But if one of us leaves, the other looks like a fool:
Some meet our families, and join right in;
Saying their family too, and more than friends:
Some we grew up with others we acquired later on;
But if you get a BFF the bond is strong:
Some friends or true, some friends are fake;
Others come around, when it's much too late:
Some embarrasses you, and call you out;
Then you find out, what they're really about:
Some feed you, clothe you, and even give you their last;
And won't treat you different, when you out of cash:
But you have to be careful, because some of them want's your life;
They'll take your man, are steel your wife:
If you don't take the time to get to know them first;
You end up seeing them, at their very worst:
We all have issues, some dark with shame;
So, don't call everyone your friend, just because
they know your name:
We have friends from the neighborhood, some from church, others
from work, some we knew from school:
They can't all be in your circle, that's just the rules:
So try to limit it to, one or two;
That'll always love you, regardless of what you do:
Some are laid back, and have battle scars;
Yet they're honest, and very loyal:
Others are restless, and hardly ever chill;
But their your friends, so you learned to deal:
We all need someone, if just to talk too;
To share our day, or see us through:
Friends come in all shapes and form;
Cheering in the good times, and comforting during the storm:
It was never intended for us to be by ourselves;
To be isolated from everyone else:
We all need someone to love, and talk things out;
And that's what friends are all about:

New Life...

Blessed is the arms of a mother holding her new life;
She chooses to bring him back to
Our Lord and Savior Jesus Christ:
She nurses him, and bond with him in the first few hours;
But she also knows that one day he'll need the Holy Ghost power:
She appreciates the gift that she holds in her hands;
She knows that she must bring him back to God, for
his perfect plan:
In the first couple of months she brings him to church
for his christening;
She invites his close family so they also be listening:
An anointed clergyman will pray, and lay hands over the child;
In order to protect him through Jesus Grace for a while:
Trust that his mother shall return him to church;
To ward off any demonic spirits, or unwanted curse:
She understands the important job that God has
bestowed upon her;
She teaches him God's word, right from the start:
Blessed is her child who's filled with God's grace;
She's knows in this world, there'll be challenges to face:
She teaches him that God gives us our daily bread;
Through studying Gods word is how we're feed:
She raises him up with strong Christian values;
She disciplines him accordingly, if she has too:

Blessed is the mother, when her child cries for her;
Jesus is with him, yet his mother's still there:
Wanting desperately always to break his fall;
However, Jesus is a comforter, he's here for us all:
She's guides him closely throughout his life:
They'll separate when he becomes a man, and takes a wife:
No worry come before her, because she raised him right;
She's knows he'll also bring his family to Jesus's light:
Now the cycle continues for the next generation;
And they're all cover under Jesus blood, from
God's beautiful creation:
Thank you, Jesus, for your New life, New life, and
New Life to Come;
Blessed to be them all, from Our Father's Love:

Passion...

Passion, the heart burst into a song, for a
love story that never exist;
From that first touch, or the very last kiss:
Deeply I hold you next to my heart;
Our souls together shall never part:
Longing for the gentle night breeze;
Embracing your presence, keeps me pleased:
Living strongly, for my true desire;
Chasing dreams, my eyes admire :
My heart is here all complex and weak;
Needing your love, just to speak:
Melting me softly, with your touch;
My mind is soaring, from its rush:
Climbing to the peak of a mountain height;
My chest pounding, with the delight:
Searching for the right words to say;
Wandering hopelessly, through my day:
Feeling the pressure of your thoughts;
Returning my love, this I doubt:
Endless possibilities, will never fade;
Ultimate decisions, to be made:
My life strives only to share with yours;
Your hope to love me, is the final score:
Desperately wanting, it not to end;
Whatever you say, you'll be my friend:

JACQUELINE JAMES

POETRY WITH A TWIST

Chapter 6

Special Dedication

1. 47 years of Love
2. Grammie-son
3. Magic girl
4. My 1st
5. Grandmother
6. 2 Hearts
7. What a friend
8. Celebration
9. Disguised
10. Miracle son
11. God Bless
12. Mother
13. Chosen
14. Breaking bridges

47 years of love…

From birth to three, you loved, nurtured, and cared for me;
From 4 to 5 you allowed me to see the world through
my own eyes;
I'm in school from 6 to 10 learning and growing and
making lots of friends:
From 11 to 13 you saw my innocent rise;
Then from 14 to 15 oh what a surprise!
Now I give birth to a beautiful daughter;
And you let me know, I was just a child -who needed her mother:
You continue to support me and mine, through
good and hard times:
Even through a struggle, you keep a smile on your face;
At age 21 I moved out of your house with knowledge and self-
respect all from your good grace:
Now I'm a young adult starting a family of my own;
Facing challenging situations, when times got difficult you were
there to remind me I was not alone:
Mistake after mistake and some very bad choices,
I was desperate and lonely wanting for it all to end;
You came to me praying, saying "baby it ain't over cause you got
me as your mother, and Jesus as your friend: In all the confusion
you help me to see;

Jacqueline James

That it was trials and tribulations molded me
into the woman I needed to be:
Through marriage after marriage and in my
darkest hour
I always knew-when all else fails, I can call on my mama!
Happy Mother's Day celebrating 47 years of love!!!!

Grammie-son...

It's a very special feeling to have a grandson;
Who's always loyal and worthy to love:
When you came in this world, I was right there;
I held you close to my heart, so you'll know I cared:
You gripped my finger, as you opened your eyes;
You knew I was yours, and you did not cry:
The feelings of pleasure overwhelmed my heart;
I fell in love with you, right from the start:
I walked you across the room, for your mama to see;
Her beautiful baby-boy, we both were pleased:
Tears of Joy gently ran drown my face;
My grandson was here, through God's good grace:
When you were a baby, I took care of you;
I feed you, played with you, and changed you too:
When you came to visit, you slept in my bed;
You laid across my chest, and you laid across my head:
You use to lay on my chest, and grab my face for a kiss;
Those precious memories, I'll always miss:
You were so fun, lovable and sweet;
I took you around, for my friends to meet:
As a child, you were always good;
You followed the rules, just like you should;
You grew taller than me, but that's ok;
Cause you still bend drown to hug and kiss me, to this day:

Jacqueline James

You're very humble, and that works out fine for me;
Many doors will open in your favor, if you continue to be:
I knew right off, you'll be popular in school;
Everyone wants to be your friend, cause you're pretty cool:
Now you're growing up, to become a nice young man;
You'll soon be making decision on your own, because you can:
I'll be right here with you, cause I don't what to
miss out on any of the fun;
I love dearly, cause you're my first -and only grandson:
Dedicated to:
Tyler Taran Kedrick Griffin

Magic-girl...

Little magic girl,
Oh, how you changed my world:
I was having fun and running wild;
The last thing I was expecting, was another child:
You where number 5 the last on my list;
Which made it hard to resist, your little kiss:
I was doing some things, I had no business doing;
And I knew if I didn't stop, our lives would be ruined:
When I got pregnant with you, my life instantly changed;
Your aunt was so tickled, she clothed me, fed me, and
even gave you- your name:
When you were born, my activities couldn't remain the same;
I refuse to have you grow up without a mother,
hurt and filled with shame:
So, I turned my life around, and it was all for the best;
Not only did it help you, is save the rest:
I must admit, there was some intervention;
When the 'State' stepped, in I had to pay attention:
I could've have given up anything my house,
my money, or my car;
But when authorities were talking about taking away my children,
that was going too far:

I did want it took, to keep you safe in my arms;
Cause your little magical self-turned on the charm:
And you're still a little 'sweetie', right to this day;
Smart as a 'whip' and I'm proud to say:
I'll love you Jeannie magic for the rest of my days:

My First...

You're an awesome daughter, and a wonderful 'Mother';
I wouldn't trade you for the world, I wouldn't want no other:
I'm glad you're mama's first born child;
Cause I could love you for a longer while:
I had you when I was so very young;
We grew up together, I have lots of fun:
I enjoyed the days I spent with you;
I keep them as precious memories
And I hope you do too:
Even though a lot of your time was spent with my mother;
She was trying to make up for losing her daughter:
Eventually you got other sisters and brothers;
But, you're very special because you were
the first born to your mother:
Now you're an adult with a daughter of your own;
I still see you as my baby, even though you're grown:
Now you're going to understand some of the challenges
I had to go through;
And it's all so worth it, to see 'mother and daughter',
love growing true:
I love you my beautiful baby girl;
And you're extra special cause you're my first
I brought into this world:
Dedicated to:
Sherece Gecelle Whitehorn

Grandmother...

To my children, grandchildren, great grandchildren, great- great
grandchildren, my brother, and all of my family and friends please
don't you dare Cry For Me!
For I've gone to heaven, where I needed to be,
I've lived a full and wonderful life;
My Lord blessed me to be a mother and a wife:
I've worked hard, I played long;
I even travel the world abroad:
I've seen and done some marvelous things;
Some of which I'll never forget;
I watch the sunrise, and the moon go down;
None of which I'll ever regret:
I've learned a lot, and taught many,
I've cooked and shared and feed plenty.
We loved, laughed, and cried together, and
prayed until times got better.
For all the birthdays, weddings, anniversaries,
holidays, new births, that I'll miss,
I'm sending my love, great big hugs, and sealing it with a kiss:
I've lived a simple life, fill with joy, inspirations, no sorrows,
I've lived a faithful life, filled with a promise of
God's grace for tomorrow:
You'll find me in everything you look at, and
in everything you touch:

From the pictures you see, the broad games you play, and
my recipes you love so much:
The game "Trouble" was my favorite and I'm still undefeated:
You knew when you sat down to play, you were
planning on being beaten:
Sometimes I may have been difficult, and maybe even a little hard;
But after I shared, my love through discipline, eventually
I dropped my guard:
Keep my memory alive, with family gatherings, good food,
laughing, playing games, and always having
great story about me to share:
Teach our young generation how to be loyal, and
strong, yet gentle enough to care:
On November 25th, 2016 at 11:09 a.m. I was giving my wings
from our Father up above;
And the most important advice I'm leaving you with is;
Don't forget to love!!!!
Frances Virginia Ming (12-3-1917) -(11-25-2016)

2 Hearts...

My heart beating inside of you;
Symbolize the love, that was beaten for two:
My heart needed to beat through you;
And you did what it took, to see me through:
Thanks Mama for loving me inside your womb;
I only came out, because I ran out of room:
All the free meals, it was easy to stay;
But I had to be born, to become your daughter one day:
Oh, what a pleasure it's been for me;
Growing up as your daughter, especially:
I'm your forth child, and the very last one on the list;
I got all the leftovers, the hand-me-downs, but also the last kiss:
There were times when I try to run wild, and be slick;
But you were from that old-school, and put me back
in my place quick:
Thanks Mom for helping me throughout the years, find my way;
Even when I told you "I got this" you still decided to stay:
You help me, you help my children, you help my grandchildren;
I must be super spoiled, because I know I'm ruined:
I hope you continue to be there for me;
Because I love you to Infinity:
I want to be there for you, to return the favor, when you're old and
tired, and could no longer labor:

You're the Best of the Best, that's why I'm so pretty-darn smart;
Cause my heartbeat next to yours, right from the start:
Throughout the years I settle for less;
But never again, because I know I'm special - I came from the best!
Dedicated to: Jeanette Louise Whitehorn

What a friend...

Oh, what's is a friend if it's not u?
Someone who's there doing a rough time to help me through!
My friends come in all shape and fashion,
They're even willing to share their rations:
To find that special friend, I don't need to look far,
Someone to love, I found a star:
When I was down and needed a hand,
You were there for me, and made no demands:
You talked about this;
And I talked about that;
We never argue, just stated facts!
On so many levels, we both understood;
We'll stay friends forever, if we could:
With a helping hand, and listening ear;
There's no doubt how much u care:
From s**** 2 Spits you were there;
Wiping and blowing, if u dare!
What made you laugh-made me smile;
And we kept it going for a long while!

I shared my life story, you shared your no worries!
You disregard my quarantine;
And got to know me, behind the scene:
If our paths should ever cross again, I'll
always know I made a friend:
Life situations made us part;
But best-believe, you're in my heart!
Dedicated to: Melissa Mudd

Celebration...

From genuine love and dedication;
You're been our source of inspiration:
You've given your time and hard work, without
complaint or hesitation;
That's way you've earn the respect of the entire congregation:
In all your kind gesture you're stayed loyal, dedicated, positive,
and motivated;
Bringing clarity and inspiration, exceeding our exception;
We all join you in your journey, for salvation;
Given honor to God for mercy and grace for allowing our 1st lady
Mrs. Jacqueline Smith another birthday celebration:

Disguised...

Today I met an angel as a woman in disguised;
When I heard her speak I was able, to recognize;
I felt the spirit it became visible to me;
Why we were able, to connect, and become friends instantly:
She wanted my opinion about some things she had written
We share similar views, and I had to admit it:
I write in poetry, she writes in paraphrases;
We share the same message, in most cases:
As we sat there and gotten acquainted;
She shared stories that was harsh, and very tainted:
She had been defiled by the person she trusted the most;
Her husband, her soulmate, who should've been close:
She had a lot of bottled up pain, and really needed to vent;
She was pleased by my presence, but I'm
sure she was 'Heaven', sent:
She had been stuck in time, trying desperately to break free;
Never realizing embracing her passion, was the key:
She had been beaten down for so long, she lost her confidence;
It lowered her self-esteem, and even made her doubt herself:
Her work with so talented, I was very impressed;
Just being in her company, made me feel blessed:
I shared a poem I had written that was similar to hers;
When she shared her paraphrase, we were at a loss of words:

JACQUELINE JAMES

It's as if I was born behind her, to carry on where she left off;
And if she failed to do so, I needed to get the message across:
Her views were deep and filled with Christians values;
The words were powerful, and meant to help you:
Throughout life's journey, doors had been slammed in her face;
When she met me, it wasn't the case:
I embraced her immediately, because I knew her self-worth:
To deny one of God's angels, would only be a curse:
As we sit there and talked, I broke out in chills;
From the things she shared, and the truth she revealed:
It wasn't by accident, or chance that we met;
We inspired each other, and had no regrets:
Neither one of us wanted the conversation to end;
But we exchanged numbers, so we can remain friends:
Dedicated to: Shelia

Miracle son...

My miracle of a son;
He was born 1 pound & 14 ounces;
I was only six months pregnant, I could've lost him:
He came here with a lot of prayer;
His birth will forever, change my world:
The doctor said he was bleeding from his brain;
He needed several blood transfusion, for his life to remain:
They said he'll never walk or speak;
I didn't hear his voice for several weeks:
They said he would always need oxygen just to breathe:
All this bad news I couldn't believe:
With the amount of oxygen, he would surely go blind;
To care for him, will take a special kind:
Couldn't breathe, won't see, couldn't speak, or walk;
Wouldn't stop bleeding from his brain;
Now I'm in a lot of pain, all the stuff is driving me insane;
"Lord take him back, you know what's best";
"I can't handle this by myself"!
Now GOD was right there watching us go through;
Though the power of prayer he healed him too:
No man can tell me what God is capable of;
When he sends down a blessing from up above:
My son is a living witness and I'm here to testify;

Our Father is able and divine:
Oh what a wonderful Lord and Savior we serve;
The doctors couldn't believe what they observed:
I admit he had some challenging days;
But as his mother I taught him to pray:
He didn't grow up like the average child;
He had special needs, for a while:
Now he's a young man standing strong;
He was blessed from God's mercy all along:
I needed to share the story of one of God's miracles;
In Christ Our Lord nothing's too difficult:
My son graduated from High school with rest of his class;
Never reflecting on his struggling past:
Now he's completed Junior College, just waiting to
walk across the stage;
Meanwhile he enrolled in a University, cause he's
not wasting any of his days:
I'm very proud of him, I hope he realize;
If he can't hear in my voice, than he'll see it, in my eyes:
Thank you Jesus for blessing my son's life
to be full and prosperous;
He's making the best of it, though hard work and generosity:
Centilus you are an amazing young man;
Anything you set your mind to you will achieve;
Though God's Grace you must believe:
Dedicated to:
Centilus Lemont Buchanan

God Bless...

In the name of Jesus, a special prayer for my Aunt Ritha;
Lord please heal her body, from the crown of her head,
to the sole of her feet;
May your blessings extend though the people she meets:
Her body is weak, and she's very tried;
Give her reassurance Jesus, that's it's not her time:
Comfort her Lord in her time of distress;
Though God she's favored and highly blessed:
Give her strength during these troubling time;
Remind her that she's your child, and she'll be fine:
Encourage her right now in Jesus name;
With your Grace she can't remain the same:
Bring her peace in the mist of her storm;
Show her Lord that she's in your arms:
Have Mercy Lord, it's all she need;
Though our faith it's done, we all believe:
We're praying Lord that you take away her pain;
All these things we ask in Jesus name.
Thank You Jesus in advance;
Now we all can do a victory dance:

Mother...

We get all types of mother's throughout our life;
Everyone has a birth mother, some of us get a God mother, others get a stepmother, or acquire a mother-in-law;
Some even get a sister-mother:
But we're truly blessed, to have a Church Mother:
She's that mature woman, who's unlike no other:
She usually sits on the first couple of roles of the pew;
Never missing an opportunity to help me are you:
She's always available, she's always on call;
While serving the Lord, and also consoling us all:
She knows more about the bible, than I understand;
She quotes scripture effortlessly, on demand:
She's always warm and caring ,filled with charm;
She's loving and nurturing with open arms:
She invites us to her home, to eat at her table;
Servings us gracefully, while she's still able:
She's always first to testify;
About the goodness of the Lord, and she'll tell you why:
She's has a lot of knowledge, and that's for sure;
From life experiences, she had to endure:
It's great to fellowship, when she's near;
She gives good advice, and has a listening ear:
It didn't surprise me, that she worked in hospitality;
She has a gentle heart, and a lovely personality:
After listening carefully she's no stranger;
She's a very own, A.K.A. Mother Granger

Chosen...

I've never met a man quite so humble before;
He's always honorable enough to give other pastors the floor:
He's not selfish nor does he asks for more;
He teaches our congregation about intercessory prayer;
How to extend our blessings, and how to share:
I've heard him say more than once or twice;
How it's just nice-to-be-nice:
I understand what that statement mean;
All the generosity he's shown, we've all seen:
I'm sure he also faces challenging times;
But when he comes to church, he disregards his own,
only seeing yours and mine:
Our bishop we serve under is truly wise:
All of his services should be televised:
He teaches us to pray in our darkest hour;
And how to embrace our Holy Ghost power:
He keeps the sermon lively and uplifting;
Instructing us to interact, so our attention is not drifting:
He allows each member to take the mic;
In order to share God's ministry if they like:
He understands that God ministry is expressed though all forms;
From preaching, singing, dancing or even sharing poems:
I respect this man a lot, even if I haven't told him enough;
He prays for us regardless if times are good or rough:

He shared a stories about his life;
How he never expected to be a preacher, and even put up a fight:
Though God Our Father he was choose;
To share the story how Jesus rose:
He has a wonderful wife, and they have children of their own;
Who love the Lord as well, though their actions, it's shown:
His leadership is a privilege to worship under;
He's a man of integrity, it's no wonder:
The King James version is the bible we study from;
We gain clarity through God's word as we come:
He preaches the word, God knows he a holy man;
He also teaches the word, making it easy to understand:
He encourages us all, in many ways;
Helping to insure, we have brighter days:
We pray with, we eat with, and fellowship with;
When it comes to extending God's glory, he never quits:
He's truly a honor to worship with;
He's our very own,
Bishop: Melvin James Smith:

Breaking Bridges...

Breaking Bridges and Mending Hearts;
We became friends right from the start:
Even though we have some cultural differences;
We're still able to share our life experiences:
I was willing to speak and you were willing to listen;
Little did you know I was on a mission:
To acquire as many smiles as possible- that was my plan;
Because life itself has too many demands:
You fell right into the trap which was hard not to do;
I brought you good cheer, and some laughs to:
I found the strength to muscle up some breathing power;
But I must admit it was a pretty fun hour:
I appreciate the short time that we did spend;
And all the compassion you were willing to lend:
The time made a difference in my day;
Even though you tortured me in your own way:
I know you had a job to do, and you do it well!
That's why it pleases me to say," You're pretty darn swell"!
Dedicated to: Jennifer Henry

JACQUELINE JAMES

JACQUELINE JAMES

www.ingramcontent.com/pod-product-compliance
Lightning Source LLC
Chambersburg PA
CBHW071739080526
44588CB00013B/2088